Halal Home Cooking

ISMAIL AHMAD

Recipes from Malaysia's Kampungs

Marshall Cavendish
Cuisine

The publisher wishes to thank Restoran Rebung Chef Ismail for the use of their kitchen and premises throughout the photography session and Royel Departmental Store Sdn Bhd and Claycraft for the loan of their tableware.

Photographer: Suan I. Lim
Author's portrait (on page 7) by Jen

First published 2006 as Malay Heritage Cuisine
Published 2012 as Chef Ismail's Malay Heritage Cooking

This new edition 2019
Published by Marshall Cavendish Cuisine
An imprint of Marshall Cavendish International

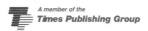

A member of the
Times Publishing Group

Other Marshall Cavendish Offices:
Marshall Cavendish Corporation, 99 White Plains Road, Tarrytown NY 10591-9001, USA • Marshall Cavendish International (Thailand) Co Ltd, 253 Asoke, 12th Floor, Sukhumvit 21 Road, Klongtoey Nua, Wattana, Bangkok 10110, Thailand • Marshall Cavendish (Malaysia) Sdn Bhd, Times Subang, Lot 46, Subang Hi-Tech Industrial Park, Batu Tiga, 40000 Shah Alam, Selangor Darul Ehsan, Malaysia

Marshall Cavendish is a registered trademark of Times Publishing Limited

National Library Board, Singapore Cataloguing in Publication Data

Name: Ismail Ahmad, 1960-
Title: Halal home cooking / Ismail Ahmad.
Description: Singapore : Marshall Cavendish Cuisine, 2019.
Identifier(s): OCN 1110583810 | ISBN 978-981-48-6845-7 (paperback)
Subject(s): LCSH: Cooking, Malay. | Cooking, Malaysian. | Formulas, recipes, etc.--Malaysia.
Classification: DDC 641.59595--dc23

Printed in Singapore

My most enduring love to those closest to my heart:

- my grandmother, *Allahyarhamah* Hajah Hawa Binti Yusof and my mother *Allahyarhamah* Hajah Mariam Binti Jabil who introduced me to the traditional Malay cuisine.

- my grandfather, *Allahyarham* Haji Jabil who imparted his wisdom to me in buying the freshest ingredients in the Tampin market, Negeri Sembilan.

- my father Haji Ahmad bin Abu, my sisters Norlia and Noorsham, my brother Fadhil and Allahyarham Abd Razak who have been most generous in their advice and encouragement.

Contents

Preface

This is where it all began. Like the taste of the forbidden fruit—my passion for the fresh produce of the orchards and the paddy fields, and my efforts in trying out the herbs and spices growing in such abundance around me—has led me to cook, cook and cook… Helping my grandmother in the kitchen has made me successful in the world of cookery. Not forgetting my grandfather though, who helped me by showing me the art of choosing the best from the sea when we were at the market.

I left my hometown in search of my dreams to become a graduate in Hotel Management and Catering with specialisation in Chef Training at the Mara University of Technology. Soon after, I joined a course with the Hilton International Kitchen Apprenticeship Programme for three years.

After getting my diploma, I worked in the food industry and became a lecturer at Taylor's College in Food Technology and Kitchen Management for two years. I was also the Chef in the industrial kitchen at KFC Holdings for seven years before becoming Executive Chef at Restoran Yasmin for a year.

Then I began a stint as a host for various cookery programmes for local television. I found a lot of satisfaction and excitement from hosting programmes like *Aroma*, *Sri Murni* and *Kuih Raya* on RTM TV1; *Hey Good Cooking*, *Wok and Roll* and *Makan Tapi Diet* on RTM TV2; *Riang Ria Bersama Cornflakes* and *Jom Masak Bersama Sri Murni* on TV3 and *Ala-Ala Kampung* on Channel 4 Astro. I also had the opportunity to host *Yok Buat Kuih Raya!* on Suria Channel, TV12, MediaCorp in Singapore.

In addition, I also joined Matrade on its tour to the United States of America, the Middle East and Europe to promote Malaysian food and products. My involvement with the Ministry of Agriculture lies in the promotion of Malaysian fruits and food in Amsterdam. I also cooked Asian food at the Lady Jessy in Cannes, South of France for two years, as well as for theatre artists at the Watermill Art Centre in South Hampton, New York for two years. With Tourism Malaysia, I travelled to Japan, South Africa, Cambodia and United Kingdom, conducting cooking demonstrations to promote Malaysian cuisine. Besides this, I am also involved in food styling and recipe creation. I act as a consultant to numerous new restaurants in the city, as well as a spokesman for a few food manufacturing companies.

My journey in life and the experiences that I have gained so far has given me the confidence to open my own restaurant called Restoran Rebung Chef Ismail with my partner Dr Sheikh Muszaphar Shukor Al-Masri. The food served in this restaurant is a tribute to the wonderfully varied tastes in food that I inherited from our forefathers. I vouch for the food and its traditional origins and the comforting taste of kampung fare from past memories.

My intention of writing this book is to document and share my culinary experience in traditional Malay cuisine, an invaluable national treasure, with our future generations. I hope that all these traditional recipes will not disappear in time. The 72 recipes showcased in this book is simple to follow and will not disappoint you. I have great hopes that this book will assist readers in trying out our traditional cuisine without fuss, and they in turn will teach their children and grandchildren so that they too may come to appreciate this national treasure of ours.

This book would not have come to fruition without the cooperation, assistance and encouragement from my partner Dr Sheikh Muszaphar and all our staff at Restoran Rebung, in particular, Normah, Azizah, Haji Ismail, Nor, Bam-Bam and Ajil. Of course, not forgetting 'Mummy' Chef Florence Tan who encouraged me tirelessly to complete the compilation of this book. To all these people and also my fans and viewers of my cookery programmes on television who have been waiting patiently for this book, I owe you my heartfelt thanks. Finally, I would like to take this opportunity to convey my apologies for any shortcomings that may be found in this book.

Ismail Ahmad

About The Author

Dato Chef Ismail Ahmad graduated from Mara University of Technology in Hotel Management and Catering, specialising in Chef Training. He worked in the food and beverage industry for several years before becoming Executive Chef at Restoran Yasmin.

Today, Chef Ismail is a familiar face on cookery shows in Malaysia and Singapore, including *Aroma*, *Sri Murni*, *Yok Buat Kuih Raya!* and *Ala-ala Kampung*. Appointed Malaysian Food Ambassador by Tourism Malaysia, he represents his country at international culinary events and promotes its cuisine.

At the Hospitality Asia Platinum Awards 2005–2006, Chef Ismail was awarded Excellence in Hospitality Personality Chef of the Year and Excellence in Hospitality Personality Malay Cuisine Chef. His restaurant, Restoran Rebung Chef Ismail, was awarded the Award for Excellence, Best Asian Cuisine Restaurant in the same year. It has also been nominated several times for Best Malay Restaurant at the Time Out KL Food & Drink Awards.

COCONUT MILK RICE NORTHERN STYLE
NASI LEMAK UTARA

INGREDIENTS

1 kg rice, washed and drained

200 ml coconut cream, extracted from 1 grated skinned coconut

1.3 litre water

4-cm knob ginger, peeled and sliced

2 stalks lemon grass, bruised

1 screwpine (pandan) leaf, knotted

3 cloves garlic, peeled and sliced

5 shallots, peeled and sliced

1 Tbsp fenugreek seeds

1 Tbsp black peppercorns

$^{1}/_{2}$ tsp salt

METHOD

Place rice, coconut cream, water, ginger, lemon grass, screwpine leaf, garlic, shallots, fenugreek seeds, black pepper and salt in an electric rice cooker. Stir well.

Switch on the rice cooker and cook until rice is done.

Fluff the rice before serving.

NOTE

This rice may be served with the following accompaniments: boiled egg, fried peanuts (groundnuts), fried dried anchovies, prawn sambal, squid sambal and fried water convolvulus (*kangkung*).

GRILLED AUBERGINE SALAD
LAWAR TERUNG

INGREDIENTS

2 aubergines (eggplants/ brinjals), long variety

1 onion, peeled and sliced

5 bird's eye chillies (*cili padi*), sliced

250 ml coconut cream, extracted from 1 grated coconut

1/2 tsp kalamansi juice

Salt to taste

FINELY GROUND

3 red chillies

3 tsp dried prawns (shrimps), soaked and drained

3 dried chillies, soaked to soften

1 tsp black peppercorns

METHOD

Grill aubergines on a charcoal grill until done. Peel and cut into 2-cm lengths. Set aside to cool.

Mix ground ingredients in a bowl until well-combined. Add onion and bird's eye chillies, coconut cream, kalamansi juice and salt. Stir well.

Add grilled aubergines and toss until well-coated. Serve immediately.

NOTE

If desired, you can substitute aubergines with:
banana bud (*jantung pisang*) that has been blanched until tender, or finely sliced boiled beef grilled in the oven at 160°C for 10 minutes, or peeled young horse mangoes (*bacang*) that has been finely shredded, or sliced cucumber.

SYAWAL RICE
NASI LAMBAIAN SYAWAL

INGREDIENTS

1 kg basmati rice, washed and drained

5 Tbsp ghee (clarified butter)

4 cloves

4 cardamom pods

6-cm length cinnamon stick

1 star anise

1/2 tsp cumin seeds

100 g masoor dhall, soaked for 20 minutes and drained

100 g mung dhall, soaked for 20 minutes and drained

100 g urad dhall, soaked for 20 minutes and drained

1.5 litres water

Fried cashew nuts for garnishing

SLICED

1 onion, peeled

3 cloves garlic, peeled

4-cm knob ginger, peeled

FINELY GROUND

5 onions, peeled

4 cloves garlic, peeled

4-cm knob ginger, peeled

METHOD

Heat the ghee in a pan over medium heat.

Fry cloves, cardamom, cinnamon stick, star anise and cumin seeds until fragrant. Add the sliced ingredients and stir until golden brown.

Stir in the ground ingredients and fry for 3 minutes. Add all the dhalls. Stir-fry for 3 minutes and pour in the water.

Stir well and transfer all into an electric rice cooker and bring to the boil. Add rice and cook until rice is done.

Garnish with fried cashew nuts and serve.

NOTE
The amount of water used would depend on the type of rice used.

From top: Syawal Rice; Syawal Beef.

SYAWAL BEEF
DAGING SINARAN SYAWAL

INGREDIENTS

1 kg topside beef, cut into
   4 x 4 x 1-cm pieces

500 ml water

6 Tbsp + 2 Tbsp
   dark soy sauce

500 ml + 60 ml cooking oil

3 Tbsp brown sugar

50 g tamarind pulp, mixed
   with 3 Tbsp water,
   squeezed and juice
   strained

Sugar and salt to taste

2 red chillies, halved
   lengthwise

2 green chillies, halved
   lengthwise

1 onion, peeled and sliced
   into rings

COARSELY GROUND

7 red chillies, large

20 shallots, peeled

6 cloves garlic, peeled

4-cm knob mature ginger,
   peeled

METHOD

In a pot, put beef, water and 6 tablespoons of dark soy sauce. Cook over medium heat and allow to boil until beef is tender.

Remove the beef and set aside the beef stock.

Heat 500 ml cooking oil in a frying pan (skillet) and fry cooked beef until golden brown. Remove from heat and set aside.

Heat 60 ml cooking oil in a pot and fry ground ingredients until oil separates.

Add brown sugar, 2 tablespoons of dark soy sauce and beef stock. Simmer over low heat until gravy thickens.

Add fried beef and tamarind juice. Season with salt and sugar to taste.

Stir and turn over occasionally. Add red and green chillies and sliced onions and cook until gravy thickens. Turn off the heat and serve.

NOTE
Syawal is the 10th month in the Islamic calendar. Muslims all over the world celebrate this month to mark the end of the fasting month of Ramadan.

RICE WITH FISH CURRY
NASI BERLAUK

INGREDIENTS

1 kg rice, washed and drained

1.3 litres water

125 ml cooking oil

1 tsp fenugreek seeds

4 Tbsp fish curry powder

1 tsp ground turmeric

250 ml coconut cream, extracted from 1 grated coconut

1.5 kg Spanish mackerel (*ikan tenggiri*), cut into 6 pieces

3 pieces dried sour fruit (*asam gelugur*)

Salt to taste

4 red chillies, slit lengthwise with ends intact

1 cucumber, small-sized, peeled and sliced

FINELY GROUND

10 dried chillies, boiled to soften

5 shallots, peeled

2 cloves garlic, peeled

5-cm knob ginger, peeled

METHOD

Place rice and water in an electric rice cooker and cook until rice is done.

Heat cooking oil in pot over medium heat. Fry fenugreek seeds until fragrant and add ground ingredients. Stir-fry until aromatic.

Add fish curry powder and ground turmeric. Stir well until oil separates.

Add coconut cream, fish and dried sour fruit. Season with salt and leave to boil.

Add red chillies, stir and turn off the heat.

Serve fish curry with rice, cucumber slices and spicy shrimp paste (*sambal belacan*).

NOTE
The amount of water used would depend on the type of rice used.

SPICY CHICKEN SOUP
SUP AYAM PEDAS

INGREDIENTS

625 ml coconut milk, extracted from 1 grated coconut and 625 ml water

250 ml water

3 stalks lemon grass, sliced

2 sprigs coriander leaves (cilantro) with roots, finely sliced

6 bird's eye chillies (*cili padi*), torn into pieces

2-cm knob young galangal, peeled and finely sliced

500 g chicken meat, diced

1 chicken stock cube

2 Tbsp fish sauce (*nampla*)

100 g oyster mushrooms

Salt to taste

3 Tbsp lime juice

METHOD

Place coconut milk, water, lemon grass, coriander leaves and roots, bird's eye chillies and galangal in a pot. Bring to the boil over medium heat.

Add chicken meat, stir and cook until chicken is tender. Stir in chicken stock cube, fish sauce and oyster mushrooms.

Season with salt to taste. Reduce heat and add lime juice.

NOTE

If coconut milk is not available, you may substitute it with evaporated milk.

This dish can be garnished with coriander leaves (cilantro) and sweet basil leaves (*daun selasih*) before serving.

From top: Spicy Chicken Soup; Rice with Fish Curry and spicy shrimp paste.

ULAM VEGETABLE KERABU RICE
NASI KERABU ULAM

INGREDIENTS

500 g rice

750 ml water

150 g chub mackerel (*ikan kembung*), grilled until done and flaked

SPICY SAMBAL SAUCE (COMBINED)

5 shallots, peeled and thinly sliced

4-cm knob ginger, peeled and thinly sliced

2 Tbsp brown sugar

1 stalk lemon grass, thinly sliced

7 red chillies, finely pounded

Salt and sugar to taste

ULAM VEGETABLES

1 cucumber, about 300 g, cored and thinly sliced lengthwise

200 g long beans, thinly sliced

5 sprigs polygonum leaves (*daun kesum*), finely sliced

1 stalk torch ginger bud (*bunga kantan*), thinly sliced

70 g bean sprouts, tailed

100 g cabbage, thinly sliced

BUDU SAUCE (COMBINED AND BOILED)

250 ml Kelantanese fish sauce (*budu*)

2 Tbsp brown sugar

1 stalk lemon grass, thinly sliced

5 shallots, peeled and thinly sliced

3 cloves garlic, peeled and thinly sliced

1 Tbsp tamarind pulp, mixed with 300 ml water, squeezed and juice strained

METHOD

Wash the rice and place in an electric rice cooker. Add water and cook until rice is done.

Add fish flakes to the cooked rice and mix well.

Serve steaming hot rice with spicy sambal sauce, *ulam* vegetables and *budu* sauce.

NOTE

For presentation purposes, the fish is not flaked and mixed in with the rice according to the method.

Ulam is a group of vegetables and herbs that are eaten raw with various types of chilli or sambal dips by the Malays. These vegetables and herbs can also be cooked.

Kerabu is a type of Malay salad which is made up of vegetables, roasted grated coconut and spices.

To whet your appetite, this *ulam* vegetable rice can also be served with boiled salted egg.

STUFFED CHILLIES
SOLOK LADA

INGREDIENTS

5 green chillies, slit lengthwise and seeded

5 red chillies, slit lengthwise and seeded

350 ml coconut cream, extracted from 1^1/$_2$ grated skinned coconuts

100 ml water

Salt and sugar to taste

FILLING (FINELY GROUND)

350 g chub mackerel (*ikan kembung*) meat, boiled

4 shallots, peeled

8 Tbsp grated skinned coconut

10 black peppercorns

METHOD

Stuff green and red chillies with filling until full. Place all the stuffed chillies in a pot.

Mix coconut cream with water and season with salt and sugar to taste. Pour into the pot filled with stuffed chillies.

Boil over medium heat until chillies are cooked and gravy thickens.

Serve with steamed white rice.

WEDDING RICE
NASI ORANG KAHWIN

INGREDIENTS

250 g ghee (clarified butter)

1.3 litres water

125 ml evaporated milk

Salt to taste

1 kg basmati rice, washed and drained

SPICES

1 star anise

3 cloves

3 cardamom pods

6-cm length cinnamon stick, broken into pieces

FINELY GROUND

3.75-cm knob ginger, peeled

6 shallots, peeled

4 cloves garlic, peeled

METHOD

Heat ghee in a pot.

Fry the spices until aromatic. Add the ground ingredients and stir well. Stir-fry until fragrant.

Stir in water, evaporated milk and season with salt to taste.

Add rice, stir and leave until liquid has been absorbed.

Reduce heat, stir well and cook until rice is done.

NOTE

If preferred, the rice can be garnished with chopped Chinese celery, crisp-fried shallots and crispy fried chicken liver before serving.

BEEF IN SPICY SOY SAUCE
DAGING MASAK ORANG MINYAK

INGREDIENTS

125 ml cooking oil

4 cloves garlic, peeled and thinly sliced

8 shallots, peeled and thinly sliced

2 Tbsp dried chilli paste

2 sprigs curry leaves

2 Tbsp dark soy sauce

2 Tbsp meat curry powder

1 Tbsp tamarind pulp, mixed with 4 Tbsp water, squeezed and juice strained

125 ml coconut cream, extracted from 1/2 grated coconut

1 kg beef, thinly sliced

Salt and sugar to taste

METHOD

Heat cooking oil in a deep pan. Add garlic and shallots and fry until fragrant. Stir in dried chilli paste, curry leaves, dark soy sauce, meat curry powder, tamarind juice and coconut cream.

Add the beef and a little water if gravy is too thick.

Cook until meat is tender and gravy thickens. Season with salt and sugar to taste.

Serve with steamed white rice.

TERENGGANU DAGANG RICE
NASI DAGANG TERENGGANU

INGREDIENTS

1 kg Thai rice, washed and soaked in water for 2 hours

500 g glutinous rice, washed and soaked in water for 6 hours

500 ml coconut cream, extracted from 2 grated skinned coconuts

10 shallots, peeled and thinly sliced

4-cm knob ginger, peeled and thinly sliced

2 tsp fenugreek seeds

$1/2$ tsp salt

METHOD

Combine Thai and glutinous rice until well-mixed. Place in a steaming tray and steam for 20 minutes over rapidly boiling water.

Meanwhile combine coconut cream, shallots, ginger and fenugreek seeds. Mix well and add salt to taste.

When rice mixture is cooked, dish out into a large bowl. Add coconut mixture to the rice and stir until well-combined. Leave aside for 10 minutes. Return to a steaming tray and steam for another 10 minutes.

Serve rice with Tuna in Spicy Coconut Milk Gravy (see following recipe) and other accompaniments as desired.

NOTE

Terengganu is one of the states in the federation of Malaysia. It is situated at the east coast of Peninsular Malaysia.

Dagang rice is a signature dish in Terengganu.

TUNA IN SPICY COCONUT MILK GRAVY
GULAI IKAN TONGKOL

INGREDIENTS

1 kg tuna, sliced into
   2-cm thick slices

500 ml + 250 ml water

3 pieces dried sour fruit
   (*asam gelugur*)

3 tsp coarse salt

2 Tbsp fish curry powder

1 Tbsp kurma curry powder

3 Tbsp dried chilli paste

125 ml cooking oil

250 ml coconut cream,
   extracted from 1 grated
   coconut

1/2 tsp salt

1/2 tsp sugar, or to taste

THINLY SLICED

2-cm knob ginger, peeled

8 shallots, peeled

4 cloves garlic, peeled

METHOD

TO PREPARE THE FISH

A day before making this dish, boil tuna with 500 ml water, dried sour fruit and coarse salt until fish is cooked. Leave fish and stock to cool separately and keep aside.

TO COOK THE GRAVY

Combine fish and kurma curry powders with dried chilli paste in a bowl and stir thoroughly.

Heat cooking oil in a pan and fry sliced ingredients until golden brown. Add curry-and-chilli paste and stir-fry until well-cooked and fragrant.

Add boiled tuna together with the stock. Stir and bring to the boil.

Pour in coconut cream and 250 ml water and leave to boil.

Season with salt and sugar. Reduce heat and allow to simmer for 5 minutes. Serve with Terengganu Dagang Rice (see previous recipe).

NOTE
This dish can also be served with sliced cucumber.

From left: Terengganu Dagang Rice; Tuna in Spicy Coconut Gravy.

From top: Ghee Rice Kampung Folk Style; Chicken Curry.

GHEE RICE KAMPUNG FOLK STYLE
NASI MINYAK ORANG KAMPUNG

INGREDIENTS

2 Tbsp ghee (clarified butter)

3 Tbsp coconut oil

3 cloves

8-cm length cinnamon stick

5 cardamom pods

3 star anise

10 shallots, peeled and
thinly sliced

4-cm knob ginger, peeled
and thinly sliced

3 cloves garlic, peeled and
thinly sliced

2 screwpine (pandan) leaves,
knotted

1.3 litres water

1 kg basmati rice, washed
and drained

125 ml evaporated milk

175 ml tomato sauce

1 tsp salt

METHOD

Heat ghee and coconut oil in a deep pan over medium heat. Fry cloves, cinnamon stick, cardamom, star anise, shallots, ginger and garlic together with pandan leaves until fragrant.

Add water and bring to the boil.

Stir in rice, evaporated milk and tomato sauce. Mix well and season with salt.

When the liquid is about to dry up, reduce heat and cook until rice is done.

NOTE
This rice can be garnished with crisp-fried shallots and fried cashew nuts before serving.

CHICKEN CURRY
GULAI AYAM

INGREDIENTS

1 chicken, about 1.5 kg, cut into 12 pieces

Salt for cleaning chicken

6 Tbsp cooking oil

250 ml coconut cream, extracted from 2 grated coconuts

750 ml water

500 g potatoes, peeled and halved

4 red chillies

Salt and sugar to taste

FINELY GROUND

2 stalks lemon grass, sliced

8 shallots, peeled

4 cloves garlic, peeled

2.5-cm knob ginger, peeled

1.25-cm knob fresh turmeric, peeled

2 Tbsp dried chilli paste

METHOD

Rub chicken pieces with salt and rinse with water. Set aside.

Heat cooking oil in a pan over medium heat and fry ground ingredients until fragrant.

Add chicken, turning over constantly, and allow to simmer for 5 minutes.

Pour in coconut cream and water. Stir well and add potatoes. Bring to the boil until chicken is tender and potatoes are soft. Add red chillies.

Season with salt and sugar to taste and stir. Simmer until gravy thickens.

Turn off the heat and serve.

ULAM VEGETABLE RICE
NASI ULAM

INGREDIENTS

Salt to taste

1 kg cooked rice, cooled

FINELY GROUND

125 g dried prawns
(shrimps), soaked to soften

8 shallots, peeled

50 g dried shrimp paste
(*belacan*) powder

100 g pounded roasted
grated coconut (*kerisik**)

50 ml lime juice

ULAM VEGETABLES
(FINELY SLICED)

50 g Indian pennywort
(*daun pegaga*)

50 g water dropwort
(*daun selom*)

50 g *ulam raja***

50 g polygonum leaves
(*daun kesum*)

1 stalk torch ginger bud
(*bunga kantan*)

METHOD

Season ground ingredients well with salt.

Combine *ulam* vegetables, ground ingredients and rice.
Mix thoroughly.

Place on a serving dish.

NOTE

* *Kerisik* is made by dry-frying grated coconut until golden brown. Then
the coconut is pounded or ground in an electric mill until fine and oily.

** There is no common name for *ulam raja* but its scientific name is
cosmos caudatus Kunth.

Ulam vegetable rice is best served cold.

LOTUS SEED GLUTINOUS RICE
NASI PULUT BIJI TERATAI

INGREDIENTS

6 Tbsp cooking oil

2 Tbsp chopped peeled garlic

10 dried Chinese mushrooms, soaked overnight and finely sliced

1 kg glutinous rice, soaked overnight and drained

30 lotus seeds, soaked, split into two and green core removed

10 dried chestnuts, soaked overnight

50 g crisp-fried shallots

1 Tbsp chicken stock granules

2 Tbsp oyster sauce

1 Tbsp dark soy sauce

1 tsp sesame oil

Salt to taste

METHOD

Bring water in a steamer to the boil.

Heat cooking oil in a pan over medium heat. Fry garlic and Chinese mushrooms until fragrant.

Add glutinous rice and stir thoroughly. Add lotus seeds, chestnuts, shallots, chicken stock, oyster sauce, dark soy sauce, sesame oil and salt to taste.

Stir-fry until well-combined. Remove from heat and divide the rice mixture into small heatproof bowls and compress.

Arrange the bowls in a steamer tray and steam for 45 minutes until rice is fully cooked.

Remove glutinous rice from bowls and serve.

NOTE
This dish is not a Malay heritage dish, but it is one of my favourites nonetheless.

GRILLED SPICY CHICKEN
AYAM PERCIK

INGREDIENTS

$^1/_2$ tsp dried shrimp paste (*belacan*) powder

500 ml coconut cream, extracted from 2 grated coconuts

Salt and sugar to taste

2 Tbsp rice flour, mixed with 6 Tbsp water

1 chicken, about 1.5 kg, skinned and cut into 4 pieces and scored

FINELY GROUND

8 shallots, peeled

3 cloves garlic, peeled

METHOD

TO PREPARE THE COCONUT SAUCE

Combine ground ingredients, shrimp paste powder and coconut cream until well-mixed. Season with salt and sugar to taste. Place into a cooking pot and bring to the boil over low heat.

Add rice flour mixture and stir well until sauce thickens. Remove from heat. Set aside a small portion of sauce for serving.

TO GRILL THE CHICKEN

Prepare the charcoal grill.

Arrange chicken pieces on a grill and grill over hot charcoal.

Baste chicken pieces with coconut sauce and grill until chicken is tender and burn marks appear on chicken by turning over and constantly basting with coconut sauce.

TO SERVE

Line serving dish with a banana leaf and place the prepared chicken on top.

Pour reserved coconut sauce on chicken and garnish with carved cucumber and tomato skin rose.

NOTE

Use lemon grass that has been crushed at the bulb portion to baste the coconut sauce on the chicken. You may also use a few pandan leaves which are knotted and shredded to get the fragrance of either the lemon grass or pandan leaves on the chicken.

Chicken can also be grilled in the oven. Ensure oven door is open while grilling chicken.

PRAWN AND LEMON GRASS CURRY
GULAI UDANG SERAI

INGREDIENTS

1 kg prawns (shrimps), medium-sized

3 shallots, peeled and sliced

3 cloves garlic, peeled and sliced

3 stalks lemon grass, bruised

125 ml water

1 piece dried sour fruit (*asam gelugur*)

250 ml coconut milk, extracted from 1/2 grated coconut and 250 ml water

2 red chillies, halved lengthwise

2 green chillies, halved lengthwise

2 turmeric leaves, torn into pieces

Salt to taste

SPICES

1 Tbsp bird's eye chilli (*cili padi*) paste

1 Tbsp dried chilli paste

1 tsp fresh turmeric paste

METHOD

Remove prawn feelers and legs. Rub prawns with salt and rinse with water.

Put prawns, spices, shallots, garlic, lemon grass and water in a pot. Stir well.

Add dried sour fruit slice and bring to the boil over medium heat until prawns change colour.

Pour in half of the coconut milk, stir and reduce heat. Leave to simmer for a while.

Add red and green chillies and turmeric leaves.

Season with salt to taste and pour in remaining coconut milk.

Lower the heat and simmer for a few minutes and continue to stir. Turn off the heat and serve.

NOTE

Always continue to stir when cooking prawn or crab in coconut milk curries. The correct way to do so is to scoop gravy from the centre of the pot and pour it back into the centre using a ladle. Make sure the coconut milk does not separate. If that happens, add more coconut milk and salt and repeat the scooping and pouring process.

BRIYANI RICE
NASI BRIYANI

INGREDIENTS

2 Tbsp ghee (clarified butter)

6 Tbsp corn oil

1 star anise

4 cloves

5-cm length cinnamon stick

50 g briyani spice powder

1.5 kg basmati rice, washed and drained

1.5 litres water

125 ml evaporated milk

Salt to taste

SLICED

2 onions, peeled

3-cm knob mature ginger, peeled

3 cloves garlic, peeled

3 tomatoes

FINELY GROUND

8 shallots, peeled

2 cloves garlic, peeled

2-cm knob mature ginger, peeled

GARNISH

100 g cashew nuts, fried until crispy and drained

120 g yellow raisins, fried and drained

METHOD

Heat ghee and corn oil in a pot over medium heat. Fry sliced ingredients until golden brown followed by star anise, cloves and cinnamon stick. Add ground ingredients and stir-fry until fragrant.

Stir in briyani spice powder and add rice. Pour in water, evaporated milk and salt to taste. Stir well.

Transfer rice into an electric rice cooker and cook until rice is done.

Garnish with cashew nuts and raisins before serving.

NOTE

Stir the rice mixture in the electric cooker before the liquid has been absorbed.

Basmati rice can be substituted with rice that is not too starchy. Amount of water required for the rice would depend on the type of rice used.

From top: Briyani Rice; Chicken Kuzi.

CHICKEN KUZI
KUZI AYAM

INGREDIENTS

1 chicken, about 1 kg, cut into 12 pieces

6 saffron strands

125 ml cooking oil

4 Tbsp ghee (clarified butter)

1 onion, peeled and sliced

5 cloves garlic, peeled and sliced

3-cm knob ginger, peeled and sliced

2 Tbsp *kuzi* spices (see below)

250 g tomato sauce

3 Tbsp condensed milk

125 ml evaporated milk

125 ml water

Salt to taste

15 almonds, fried and drained

50 g yellow raisins, fried and drained

KUZI SPICES (FINELY GROUND)

1 tsp cumin seeds

1/2 tsp fennel seeds

1/4 tsp black peppercorns

4 cloves

3 cardamom pods

1 piece mace*

METHOD

Rub chicken with salt and saffron strands. Set aside to marinate for a few minutes.

Heat cooking oil in a pot and fry chicken until is cooked. Remove and set aside.

Heat ghee in a pan and fry onion, garlic and ginger until soft. Add *kuzi* spices and stir-fry until fragrant.

Stir in tomato sauce, condensed milk, evaporated milk and water. Stir and leave to boil.

Add fried chicken and cook until gravy thickens. Season with salt.

Sprinkle with fried almonds and raisins, and mix well.

Serve with briyani rice.

NOTE
* Mace is the vivid scarlet membrane (aril) that forms a lacy web over the seed of the nutmeg fruit.

FOUR-ANGLED BEAN KERABU
KERABU KACANG BOTOL

INGREDIENTS

15 four-angled/winged beans

125 ml lime juice

125 ml coconut cream, extracted from 1 grated coconut

Sugar and salt to taste

1 stalk lemon grass, thinly sliced

8 shallots, peeled and thinly sliced

FINELY GROUND

5 red chillies

10 bird's eye chillies (*cili padi*)

1 Tbsp dried shrimp paste (*belacan*) powder

2 Tbsp dried prawns (shrimps), soaked to soften

8 shallots, peeled

METHOD

Rub four-angled beans with a little salt, rinse and slice diagonally 0.5-cm thick. Set aside.

Mix ground ingredients with lime juice and coconut cream until well-combined. Add sugar and salt to taste.

Stir in lemon grass and shallots, and mix well.

Add four-angled beans and toss until combine. Make sure that the *kerabu* is well-flavoured with enough salt, lime juice and sugar.

NOTE
This *kerabu* will taste better with roasted grated coconut added.

DUCK EGG WITH UNRIPE MANGO CURRY
GULAI TELUR ITIK BERMANGGA MUDA

INGREDIENTS

250 ml coconut cream, extracted from 1 grated coconut

100 ml water

1 Tbsp bird's eye chilli (*cili padi*) paste

1 tsp fresh turmeric paste

2 shallots, peeled and thinly sliced

1 clove garlic, peeled and thinly sliced

1 piece dried sour fruit (*asam gelugur*)

Salt to taste

4 duck eggs

2 unripe mangoes, peeled, stoned and sliced

2 green chillies, halved lengthwise

METHOD

In a pot, combine coconut cream, water, bird's eye chili paste, turmeric paste, shallots, garlic, dried sour fruit and salt. Bring to the boil over high heat, stirring constantly to avoid oil from separating.

Reduce heat and simmer for 5 minutes. Turn off the heat and break the egg one at a time into the simmering gravy. Cook until the eggs are three-quarter cooked.

Turn on the heat and add mangoes, stir and cook until mangoes are soft. Add green chillies and season with salt to taste.

Turn off the heat and serve.

NOTE
To avoid oil from separating, cook curry over low heat and always scoop gravy from the centre of the pot and pour it back into the centre using a ladle.

COCKLE KERABU
KERABU KERANG

INGREDIENTS

300 g fresh cockle meat

1 Tbsp roasted grated
skinned coconut

125 ml coconut cream,
extracted from 1/2 grated
coconut

500 g bean sprouts, tailed

5 bird's eye chillies (*cili padi*)

2 limes, juice extracted

Salt to taste

FINELY GROUND

4 red chillies

6 shallots, peeled

1 Tbsp dried prawns
(shrimps), soaked to soften

METHOD

Combine ground ingredients, cockle meat, roasted grated
coconut and coconut cream in a bowl. Mix well.

Add bean sprouts, bird's eye chillies and mix well before
adding lime juice. Season with salt to taste – ensure that the
taste is rich and sour.

NOTE

If you prefer an extra spicy *kerabu*, add more bird's eye chillies as desired
and grind together with all the other ground ingredients.

PAHANG PATIN IN FERMENTED DURIAN GRAVY
GULAI IKAN PATIN PAHANG

INGREDIENTS

2 Tbsp fermented durian (*tempoyak*)

3 red chillies, finely pounded

6 bird's eye chillies (*cili padi*), finely pounded

4-cm knob fresh turmeric, peeled and finely pounded

1 stalk lemon grass, bruised

450 ml water

1 patin (a type of freshwater fish)*, about 1.5 kg, cut into 3-cm slices

1 tomato, wedged

1 cucumber, halved lengthwise and sliced 2-cm diagonally

1 red chilli, slit lengthwise with ends intact

1 green chilli, slit lengthwise with ends intact

1 turmeric leaf, small, torn into pieces

Salt to taste

METHOD

Mix fermented durian, pounded red chillies, bird's eye chillies, turmeric, lemon grass and water in a pot.

Bring to the boil over medium heat.

Add fish, tomato, cucumber, red and green chillies and turmeric leaf. Simmer until cooked. Season with salt.

NOTE

Pahang is one of the states in the federation of Malaysia. It is situated on the east coast of Peninsular Malaysia.

* There is no common name for patin but its scientific name is *Pangasius spp*.

Clean the fish with coarse salt and tamarind pulp to get rid of the muddy smell.

MANGO KERABU
KERABU MANGGA

INGREDIENTS

500 g unripe mangoes, peeled, stoned and shredded

1 tsp, dried prawns (shrimps) soaked to soften and ground

2 Tbsp roasted grated skinned coconut

2 Tbsp lime juice

Salt and sugar to taste

FINELY GROUND

10 bird's eye chillies (*cili padi*)

10 shallots, peeled

METHOD

In a bowl, put mangoes, dried prawns and roasted grated coconut.

Add ground ingredients and mix until well-combined.

Season with lime juice, salt and sugar to taste. Serve immediately.

GRILLED PRAWN WITH MUSHROOM SAUCE
UDANG PANGGANG BERSOS CENDAWAN

INGREDIENTS

500 g prawns (shrimps),
  feelers and legs removed
  and deveined

Salt to taste

SAUCE

1 tsp sesame oil

2 Tbsp chopped peeled
  garlic

10 bird's eye chillies
  (*cili padi*), finely chopped

3 Tbsp mushroom sauce,
  ready-to-use

1 Tbsp honey

Salt to taste

Cornflour (cornstarch)
  ½ tsp, mixed with
  250 ml water

METHOD

Marinate prawns with salt and grill in the oven with the door slightly ajar for 10–15 minutes until prawns are cooked.

To prepare the sauce, heat sesame oil in a pan over medium heat. Fry garlic, bird's eye chillies and stir well.

Add mushroom sauce, honey and salt to taste.

Reduce heat and stir in cornflour mixture. Add a little water if the sauce is too thick.

Arrange the grilled prawns closely in a serving dish and pour mushroom sauce over. Garnish as desired and serve.

NOTE

You can garnish this dish with coriander leaves (cilantro) and red chilli slices.

This dish is not a Malay heritage dish, but it is one of my favourites nonetheless.

PINEAPPLE, CUCUMBER AND CARROT PICKLE
ACAR JELATAH

INGREDIENTS

500 g pineapple

1 cucumber, about 200 g

1 carrot

4 Tbsp sugar

1/2 tsp salt

1 Tbsp vinegar or lime juice

1 onion, peeled and
   thinly sliced

3 red chillies, seeded and
   thinly sliced

METHOD

Skin the pineapple, cucumber and carrot. Cut pineapple, cucumber and carrot into thin slices as desired. Set aside.

Combine sugar, salt, vinegar or lime juice in a bowl and mix until well-combined. Set aside.

Just before serving, mix pineapple, cucumber, carrot, onion and chilli slices with vinegar mixture.

NOTE
You may add red chillies and crushed fried peanuts (groundnuts) to this pickle.

REMBAU BEEF RENDANG
RENDANG DAGING REMBAU

INGREDIENTS

30 dried chillies, boiled to soften and finely ground

20 bird's eye chillies (*cili padi*), finely ground

2 stalks lemon grass, bruised

5 shallots, peeled and thinly sliced

3 cloves garlic, peeled and thinly sliced

2 Tbsp fresh turmeric paste

1 tsp ground turmeric

2 Tbsp meat curry powder

1 kg topside beef, cut into 2 x 2 cm cubes

500 ml water

750 ml coconut milk, extracted from 3 grated coconuts and 750 ml water

Salt to taste

METHOD

Combine ground dried chillies and bird's eye chillies and lemon grass in a pot over high heat and stir well.

Add shallots, garlic, turmeric paste and ground turmeric, meat curry powder and beef. Stir-fry until well-mixed.

Add water and cook until beef is tender.

Reduce the heat, add coconut milk and allow to simmer until the gravy thickens and turns dark brown. Season with salt.

NOTE

Rembau is one of the nine districts that make up the state of Negeri Sembilan. Negeri Sembilan is one of the states in the federation of Malaysia.

This *rendang* can be served with steamed white rice or compressed rice (*ketupat*).

From top: Pineapple, Cucumber and Carrot Pickle; Rembau Beef Rendang.

Clockwise from top: Spicy and Tangy Soup; Grilled Fish with Tamarind Dip.

SPICY AND TANGY SOUP
SUP PINDANG PEDAS

INGREDIENTS

50 ml cooking oil

1 litre water

200 g prawns (shrimps), shelled and deveined

300 g chicken breast, cut into 3 x 3 cm cubes

200 g squid, cleaned and cut into rings

8 baby corn cobs, cut into halves lengthwise

2 carrots, peeled and cut into 2-cm thick slices

300 g cauliflower, cut into small florets

2 tomatoes, quartered

2 shallots, peeled and quartered

5 kaffir lime leaves (*daun limau purut*), torn into pieces

200 ml coconut cream, extracted from 1 grated coconut

FINELY GROUND

20 dried chillies, boiled to soften

20 bird's eye chillies (*cili padi*)

3-cm knob young galangal, peeled

3 stalks lemon grass, sliced

10 shallots, peeled

5 cloves garlic, peeled

SEASONING

2 tom yam stock cubes

1 anchovy stock cube

5 limes, large, juice extracted

Salt and sugar to taste

METHOD

Heat cooking oil in a pot over high heat and fry ground ingredients until fragrant.

Stir in water and bring to the boil. Reduce the heat and add prawns, chicken breast and squid followed by baby corn cobs, carrots, cauliflower, tomatoes and shallots.

Season with tom yam and anchovy stock cubes, lime juice, salt and sugar. Add kaffir lime leaves and stir well.

Pour in coconut cream, stir and leave to boil.

NOTE

Don't over cook the vegetables, chicken breast and prawns as it will soften the vegetables and harden the chicken and prawns.

This dish can also be garnished with coriander (cilantro) and sweet basil leaves (*daun selasih*) before serving.

GRILLED FISH WITH TAMARIND DIP

IKAN BAKAR AIR ASAM

INGREDIENTS

125 ml coconut cream, extracted from $3/4$ grated coconut

Salt to taste

2 banana leaves, each measuring 15 x 15 cm

1 kg chub mackerel (*ikan kembung*), cleaned with salt and tamarind pulp

FINELY GROUND

8 shallots, peeled

2 cloves garlic, peeled

METHOD

Mix the ground ingredients with coconut cream and salt until well-combined.

Line the grill or wire mesh with banana leaves.

Place fish on banana leaf and spread coconut mixture on fish.

Grill for 30 minutes in the oven grill with the oven door slightly ajar.

Serve grilled fish with Tamarind Dip with Herbs (see recipe on page 46).

TAMARIND DIP WITH HERBS
AIR ASAM BERHERBA

(See recipe for Grilled Fish with Tamarind Dip on page 45.)

INGREDIENTS

250 g tamarind pulp,
mixed with 500 ml water,
squeezed and juice
strained

125 ml lime juice

Salt and sugar to taste

FINELY GROUND

3 red chillies

6 bird's eye chillies (*cili padi*)

1 Tbsp dried shrimp paste
(*belacan*) powder

THINLY SLICED

1 onion, peeled

1 stalk torch ginger bud
(*bunga kantan*)

4 sprigs polygonum leaves
(*daun kesum*)

2 tomatoes

METHOD

Mix ground ingredients in a bowl and add tamarind juice and lime juice. Stir well. Add sliced ingredients, mix and season with salt and sugar to taste.

NOTE

You can also add shredded kaffir lime leaves (*daun limau purut*) for a fresher aroma.

SPICY WHOLE CHICKEN
AYAM GOLEK

INGREDIENTS

1 chicken, about 1.5 kg

Coarse salt for rubbing

125 ml cooking oil

2.5-cm knob galangal,
   peeled and lightly crushed

1 stalk lemon grass, bruised

1/2 tsp ground turmeric

2 tsp tamarind pulp,
   mixed with 125 ml water,
   squeezed and juice
   strained

Salt and sugar to taste

1 litre coconut cream,
   extracted from 2 grated
   coconuts

FINELY GROUND

20 shallots, peeled

5 cloves garlic, peeled

2 stalks lemon grass, sliced

10 dried chillies, boiled
   to soften

2.5-cm knob ginger, peeled

METHOD

Rub chicken with coarse salt. Wash and drain. Make several slits in the chicken breast.

Heat cooking oil in a pot big enough to fit a whole chicken and fry ground ingredients until fragrant.

Add galangal, lemon grass, ground tumeric, tamarind juice and salt and sugar to taste. Stir evenly.

Pour in coconut cream, stir and add the chicken.

Cook until gravy thickens and the chicken becomes tender.

NOTE

To enhance the flavour of the cooked chicken, thread chicken using sugar cane sticks and grill until crispy over hot charcoal or under the grill in the oven.

THAI STYLE SOUP
SUP SIAM

INGREDIENTS

120 ml cooking oil

1.5 litres water

4 tom yam stock cubes

10 bird's eye chilllies
(*cili padi*), crushed

6 kaffir lime leaves
(*daun limau purut*)

2 stalks lemon grass, bruised

1 can button mushrooms,
quartered

750 g chicken meat, cubed

300 ml evaporated milk

Salt to taste

Coriander leaves (cilantro)
for garnishing

FINELY GROUND

30 dried chillies, soaked
to soften

20 shallots, peeled

8 cloves garlic, peeled

4-cm knob young galangal,
peeled

2 stalks lemon grass, sliced

2 tsp dried shrimp paste
(*belacan*) powder

2 sprigs coriander
(cilantro) roots

3 kaffir lime leaves
(*daun limau purut*)

6 sweet basil leaves
(*daun selasih*)

1^1/$_2$ Tbsp sugar

1 chicken stock cube

METHOD

Heat cooking oil in a pot and fry ground ingredients until
aromatic while stirring slowly.

Stir in water, tom yam stock cubes, bird's eye chillies, kaffir
lime leaves and lemon grass. Bring to the boil.

Add button mushrooms and chicken. Stir and simmer for
a while.

Pour in evaporated milk and season with salt.

Garnish with coriander leaves before serving.

BITTER GOURD IN COCONUT MILK GRAVY
GULAI LEMAK PERIA

INGREDIENTS

5 bitter gourds, small variety
(*peria katak*)

Coarse salt for rubbing

2 Tbsp fish curry powder

300 g prawns (shrimps),
feelers removed

4 shallots, peeled and sliced

2 cloves garlic, peeled
and sliced

1 stalk lemon grass, bruised

1 piece dried sour fruit
(*asam gelugur*)

250 ml coconut milk,
extracted from 1/2 grated
coconut and 250 ml water

250 ml water

Sugar and salt to taste

2 kaffir lime (*daun limau
purut*) or turmeric leaves,
finely sliced

METHOD

Halve the bitter gourds lengthwise, remove the core and slice into two with ends intact. Rub with coarse salt and rinse.

In a pot, place bitter gourds, fish curry powder, prawns, shallots, garlic, lemon grass, dried sour fruit, coconut milk and water. Bring to the boil over medium heat until bitter gourds are cooked and gravy thickens.

Season with sugar and salt to taste and add kaffir lime or turmeric leaves.

PRAWN SAMBAL WITH PARKIA BEANS
SAMBAL UDANG PETAI

INGREDIENTS

250 ml cooking oil

2 Tbsp sugar

500 g prawns (shrimps), feelers removed and cleaned with salt

300 g parkia/stink beans (*petai*)

2 Tbsp tamarind pulp, mixed with 125 ml water, squeezed and juice strained

1 anchovy stock cube

6 Tbsp coconut cream, extracted from ¼ grated coconut

Salt to taste

1 onion, peeled and sliced into rings

FINELY GROUND

20 dried chillies, boiled to soften

10 shallots, peeled

1 Tbsp dried shrimp paste (*belacan*) powder

METHOD

Heat cooking oil and fry ground ingredients until fragrant. Add sugar and stir until sugar dissolves and caramelises.

Add prawns, parkia/stink beans, tamarind juice, anchovy stock cube and coconut cream. Season with salt and stir until cooked. Add onions and follow with more water if gravy is too thick.

Transfer to a bowl and serve.

From top: Bitter Gourd in Coconut Milk Gravy; Prawn Sambal with Parkia Beans.

YOUNG BANANA IN COCONUT MILK GRAVY
LEMAK PUTIH PISANG MUDA

INGREDIENTS

20 young bananas

70 g dried anchovies

20 shallots, peeled

1/2 tsp dried shrimp paste
   (*belacan*), crushed

250 ml coconut cream,
   extracted from 1 grated
   coconut

150 ml water

1 turmeric leaf, torn
   into pieces

Salt to taste

METHOD

Halve bananas lengthwise and soak in salt water for a short while to prevent discolouration.

Grind dried anchovies, shallots and dried shrimp paste until fine.

Put coconut cream, water, turmeric leaf, ground ingredients and bananas in a pot. Cook over medium heat and bring to the boil.

Reduce heat, stir slowly until gravy thickens.

Simmer until bananas are soft and season with salt.

NOTE
You may substitute dried anchovies with dried prawns (shrimps) and add black peppercorns to grind together with shallots and dried shrimp paste to make the dish spicier.

THICK BEEF CURRY
GULAI DAGING DARAT

INGREDIENTS

6 Tbsp cooking oil

2 Tbsp meat curry powder

2 Tbsp ginger juice

1 Tbsp pounded roasted grated coconut (*kerisik**)

0.5 kg beef sirloin, cut into pieces

500 ml water

1 piece dried sour fruit (*asam gelugur*)

Salt and sugar to taste

2 Tbsp Kelantanese fish sauce (*budu*)

250 ml coconut milk, extracted from 1 grated coconut and 250 ml water

FINELY GROUND

5 shallots, peeled

3 cloves garlic, peeled

2.5-cm knob ginger, peeled

METHOD

Heat cooking oil in a pan over medium heat until hot. Fry ground ingredients until fragrant.

Stir in meat curry powder and ginger juice and stir-fry until aromatic. Add pounded roasted grated coconut and reduce the heat.

Add the beef and stir until well-mixed. Pour in half of water and cook until beef is tender.

Add dried sour fruit, and salt and sugar to taste, followed by Kelantanese fish sauce.

Pour in coconut milk and remaining water. Bring to the boil.

Remove from heat and serve with steamed white rice.

NOTE
* *Kerisik* is made by dry-frying grated coconut until golden brown. Then the coconut is pounded or ground in an electric mill until fine and oily.

From top: Young Banana in Coconut Milk Gravy; Thick Beef Curry.

From top: Aubergine in Rich Curry; Smoked Beef in Thick Coconut Milk Gravy.

AUBERGINE IN RICH CURRY
PACERI TERUNG

INGREDIENTS

6 Tbsp cooking oil

5 shallots, peeled and sliced

3 cloves garlic, peeled and sliced

2.5-cm knob ginger, peeled and sliced

2 sprigs curry leaves

3-cm length cinnamon stick

3 star anise

3 cardamom pods

3 Tbsp meat curry powder, mixed with a little water into a paste

2 aubergines (eggplants/ brinjals), long variety, cut into two and halved lengthwise with ends intact

250 ml coconut milk, extracted from $1/2$ grated coconut and 250 ml water

Salt and sugar to taste

1 Tbsp pounded roasted grated coconut (kerisik*)

METHOD

Heat cooking oil in a pan and fry shallots, garlic, ginger, curry leaves, cinnamon stick, star anise and cardamom for 5 minutes.

Add meat curry powder and stir-fry for another 3 minutes.

Stir in aubergines and coconut milk. Season with salt and sugar to taste.

Pour in a little water and add pounded roasted grated coconut. Continue to cook for another 7 minutes until done.

Serve with steamed white rice and other accompanying dishes as desired.

NOTE
* Kerisik is made by dry-frying grated coconut until golden brown. Then the coconut is pounded or ground in an electric mill until fine and oily.

SMOKED BEEF IN THICK COCONUT MILK GRAVY
GULAI LEMAK DAGING SALAI

INGREDIENTS

1 kg beef sirloin, cut into
  big pieces

2 Tbsp coarse salt

20 bird's eye chillies
  (*cili padi*)

1.25-cm knob fresh turmeric,
  peeled

4 shallots, peeled and sliced

2 cloves garlic, peeled
  and sliced

2 pieces dried sour fruit
  (*asam gelugur*)

1 stalk lemon grass, bruised

500 ml water

500 ml coconut milk,
  extracted from 2 grated
  coconuts and 500 ml water

4 potatoes, peeled
  and cubed

Salt to taste

5 green chillies, halved
  lengthwise

METHOD

Score the beef pieces and rub in coarse salt.

Grill over a coal heat until beef becomes dry. Cut the grilled beef into 2.5 x 1.5 cm pieces and set aside.

Grind or pound bird's eye chillies with turmeric until fine.

In a pot, mix beef, ground ingredients, shallots, garlic, dried sour fruit, lemon grass and water. Boil over medium heat.

Add coconut milk, potatoes and salt to taste.

Stir over low heat until gravy boils. Continue to stir until gravy thickens and potatoes are soft. Add green chillies and turn off the heat.

NOTE
This dish is more delicious if it is cooked with bilimbi fruit (*belimbing buluh*), young horse mangoes (*bacang*) or *telunjuk* aubergines.

TAPIOCA SHOOT RENDANG
RENDANG PUCUK UBI

INGREDIENTS

500 ml coconut cream,
    extracted from 2 grated
    coconuts

5 shallots, peeled and thinly
    sliced

2 cloves garlic, peeled and
    thinly sliced

1 piece dried sour fruit
    (*asam gelugur*)

100 g dried salted fish,
    shredded

¹/₂ tsp ground dried chillies

¹/₂ tsp ground turmeric

500 g tapioca shoots

Salt to taste

FINELY GROUND

20 bird's eye chillies
    (*cili padi*)

1.25-cm knob fresh turmeric,
    peeled

METHOD

Place coconut cream, ground ingredients, shallots, garlic, dried sour fruit, salted fish, ground dried chilli and turmeric in a pot. Stir well.

Bring to the boil over medium heat and stir continuously until oil separates.

Add tapioca shoots and stir. Season with salt to taste. Cook until the shoots are tender.

NOTE
You may substitute dried salted fish with dried anchovies (*ikan bilis kering*).

SOY CHICKEN
AYAM SOYA

INGREDIENTS

6 Tbsp olive oil

2 onions, large, peeled and diced

1 Tbsp chopped peeled garlic

1 Tbsp chopped peeled ginger

1 Tbsp dried chilli paste

1 Tbsp preserved soy bean paste (*tau cheong*)

500 g chicken breast, deboned and cut into small cubes

200 g button mushrooms, quartered

2 Tbsp light soy sauce

2 Tbsp oyster sauce

2 Tbsp dark soy sauce

1 tsp sesame oil

250 ml soy milk

5 Tbsp soy beans, soaked overnight and coarsely pounded

1 Tbsp salt

1 Tbsp sugar

1 Tbsp liquid seasoning

1 Tbsp chicken stock granules

METHOD

Heat olive oil in a pot. Fry onion, garlic and ginger.

Add dried chilli paste and preserved soy bean paste. Stir-fry until fragrant.

Add chicken and button mushrooms and stir over high heat.

Stir in light soy sauce, oyster sauce, dark soy sauce and sesame oil. Reduce heat and pour in soy milk and pounded soy beans. Stir well.

Season with salt, sugar, liquid seasoning and chicken stock granules. Simmer until gravy thickens.

CHEF'S NOTE:
You may add cashew nuts and chopped spring onions (scallion) to this dish if desired.

This dish is not a Malay heritage dish, but it is one of my favourites nonetheless.

AUBERGINE AND SALTED FISH CURRY
GULAI TERUNG PANJANG IKAN MASIN

INGREDIENTS

400 g salted fish bones
and meat, cleaned and
soaked in water for a while
and drained

500 ml water

2 shallots, peeled and sliced

2 cloves garlic, peeled
and sliced

1 Tbsp bird's eye chilli
(*cili padi*) paste

1 tsp fresh turmeric paste

2 pieces dried sour fruit
(*asam gelugur*)

250 ml coconut milk,
extracted from $1/2$ grated
coconut and 250 ml water

3 aubergines (eggplants/
brinjals), medium-sized
long variety, cut as desired

Salt to taste

METHOD

Put water and salted fish bones and meat in a pot together
with shallots, garlic, bird's eye chilli paste, turmeric paste and
dried sour fruit. Cook over medium heat until gravy begins
to thicken.

Pour in coconut milk and stir slowly over low heat until it
boils. Add the aubergines.

Cook until aubergines are tender.

Season with salt to taste and remove from heat.

NOTE
To avoid oil from separating, cook curry over low heat and always
scoop gravy from the centre of the pot and pour it back into the centre
using a ladle.

GRILLED BEEF WITH TAMARIND DIP
DAGING BAKAR AIR ASAM

INGREDIENTS

1 kg beef sirloin

1 Tbsp coarse salt

1 banana leaf,
  measuring 30 x 30 cm

METHOD

Wash and make several slits on the beef. Rub beef evenly with coarse salt.

Place beef on grill or wire mesh lined with banana leaf.

Grill for 30 minutes over a coal heat until beef is cooked.

Remove from grill and slice as desired.

Serve with Tamarind Dip (see recipe below).

TAMARIND DIP (AIR ASAM)

INGREDIENTS

5 green chillies, sliced

10 bird's eye chillies
  (*cili padi*), sliced

10 shallots, peeled
  and sliced

2 limes, juice extracted

2 tomatoes, wedged and
  thinly sliced

3 Tbsp tamarind pulp,
  mixed with 75 ml of
  water, squeezed and juice
  strained

1 tsp dried shrimp paste
  (*belacan*) powder

100 ml water

$^1/_2$ tsp salt

METHOD

Combine all the ingredients in a bowl and mix well.

TAPIOCA SHOOT AND FERMENTED DURIAN SAMBAL
SAMBAL TEMPOYAK PUCUK UBI KAYU

INGREDIENTS

400 g fermented durian
(*tempoyak*)

2 tsp fresh turmeric paste

20 bird's eye chillies
(*cili padi*)

500 ml coconut milk,
extracted from 1 grated
coconut and 500 ml water

Salt to taste

SLICED

8 shallots, peeled

3 cloves garlic, peeled

20 parkia/stink beans (*petai*)

4 stalks lemon grass

4 green chillies

4 red chillies

500 g tapioca shoots,
leaves only

4 turmeric shoots,
leaves only

6 pumpkin shoots,
leaves only

METHOD

In a pot, combine fermented durian, turmeric paste, bird's eye chillies and coconut milk and bring to the boil over medium heat while stirring slowly.

Simmer for 5–10 minutes and continue to stir.

Add shallots, garlic, parkia/stink beans, lemon grass, and red and green chillies. Stir well.

Add tapioca, turmeric and pumpkin shoots and stir. Season with salt before turning off the heat.

NOTE
This dish is best served a day after cooking.

STINGRAY IN HOT AND SOUR GRAVY
IKAN PARI ASAM PEDAS

INGREDIENTS

500 g stingray, cut into big pieces

Coarse salt and tamarind pulp for rubbing

125 ml cooking oil

2 stalks torch ginger bud (*bunga kantan*), halved lengthwise, if desired

1 sprig polygonum leaves (*daun kesum*), leaves only

500 ml water

4 ladies' fingers, stalk discarded

2 Tbsp tamarind pulp, mixed with 125 ml water, squeezed and juice strained

Salt to taste

FINELY GROUND

10 shallots, peeled

8 Tbsp dried chilli paste

5 red chillies

2-cm knob fresh turmeric, peeled

2 tsp dried shrimp paste (*belacan*) powder

METHOD

Wash and clean stingray with salt and tamarind pulp. Rinse a few times and drain.

Heat cooking oil in a pot over high heat and fry ground ingredients until fragrant.

Reduce the heat and add stingray, torch ginger bud (if using) and polygonum leaves. Stir well. Pour in half of the water and simmer for 5 minutes.

Add ladies' fingers, the remaining water, and tamarind juice. Increase the heat. Season with enough salt. Allow to boil and turn off the heat.

From top: Tapioca Shoot and Fermented Durian Sambal; Stingray in Hot and Sour Gravy.

GRILLED HERRING
TERUBUK BAKAR

INGREDIENTS

1 herring (*ikan terubuk*),
    about 1 kg

250 ml coconut cream,
    extracted from 1 grated
    coconut

8 shallots, peeled and ground

2 cloves garlic, peeled
    and ground

Salt to taste

2 banana leaves, each
    measuring 30 x 30 cm

1 stalk lemon grass,
    thinly sliced

METHOD

Wash the fish (without removing the scales) with salt water
and drain.

Combine coconut cream with shallots and garlic and season
with a little salt.

Line the grill or wire mesh with banana leaves. Preheat oven
to 160°C.

Place fish on banana leaves and spread the coconut milk mixture
evenly on the fish. Sprinkle sliced lemon grass over the fish.

Bake for 30 minutes with the oven door slightly ajar to avoid
smoke and damage to the oven.

Serve with Tamarind Dip with Ground Chillies (see recipe below).

TAMARIND DIP WITH GROUND CHILLIES
AIR ASAM BERCILI KISAR

INGREDIENTS

1 onion, peeled and
    thinly sliced

1 stalk torch ginger bud
    (*bunga kantan*), thinly
    sliced

4 sprigs polygonum leaves
    (*daun kesum*), finely sliced

2 tomatoes, finely sliced

FINELY GROUND

3 red chillies

6 bird's eye chillies (*cili padi*)

1 Tbsp dried shrimp paste
    (*belacan*) powder

SEASONING

250 g tamarind pulp,
    mixed with 250 ml water,
    squeezed and juice
    strained

Sugar and salt to taste

METHOD

Mix all the ingredients until well-combined and serve with
grilled fish.

FISH SAUCE AND ULAM LEAVES DIP PAHANG STYLE
BUDU PAHANG

INGREDIENTS

60 ml cooking oil

250 ml Kelantanese fish sauce (*budu*)

600 ml coconut milk, extracted from 1 grated coconut and 600 ml water

THINLY SLICED

15 bird's eye chillies (*cili padi*)

5 red chillies

10 bilimbi fruits (*belimbing buluh*)

10 shallots, peeled

5 cloves garlic, peeled

5-cm knob ginger, peeled

4 stalks lemon grass

ULAM LEAVES (FINELY SLICED)

2 turmeric leaves

2 pointed pepper leaves (*daun kaduk*)

4 sprigs polygonum leaves (*daun kesum*)

METHOD

Heat cooking oil in a pan over medium heat and fry sliced ingredients until soft.

Add the Kelantanese fish sauce and coconut milk. Stir until well-combined and bring to the boil.

Add *ulam* leaves and continue to stir until dry.

Serve with grilled fish.

Clockwise from top: Grilled Herring, Tamarind Dip with Ground Chillies; Fish Sauce and Ulam Leaves Dip Pahang Style.

VEGETABLES AND BEAN CURD CURRY THAI STYLE
LODEH SIAM

INGREDIENTS

100 ml cooking oil

1 litre water

200 ml coconut cream, extracted from 1 grated coconut

2 tom yam stock cubes

1 tsp anchovy stock granules

Salt to taste

1 Tbsp lime juice

FINELY GROUND

15 bird's eye chillies (*cili padi*)

5 shallots, peeled

4 cloves garlic, peeled

1 sprig sweet basil leaves (*daun selasih*)

2 sprigs coriander leaves (cilantro) with roots

2 stalks lemon grass, sliced

3-cm knob fresh turmeric, peeled

3-cm knob galangal, peeled

3-cm knob ginger, peeled

2 tsp dried chilli paste

VEGETABLES (BLANCHED)

1/2 cabbage, medium-sized, thickly sliced

350 g long beans, cut as desired

300 g yam bean, skinned and cut into long strips

DEEP-FRIED

3 blocks firm bean curd (*tauhu*), cut as desired

250 g fermented soy bean cake (*tempe*), cut as desired

METHOD

Heat cooking oil in a pot over medium heat. Fry ground ingredients until aromatic.

Pour in water and leave to simmer for 15 minutes. Add coconut cream and stir constantly to avoid oil from separating.

Add tom yam stock cubes, anchovy stock granules and salt to taste.

Stir and allow to boil for another 15 minutes. Add lime juice.

Before serving, add blanched vegetables, fried bean curd and fermented soy bean cake. Stir well.

NASI KANDAR BEEF
DAGING NASI KANDAR

INGREDIENTS

1 Tbsp ghee (clarified butter)

6 Tbsp cooking oil

4 sprigs curry leaves

1 kg onions, peeled and thinly sliced

4 cloves garlic, peeled and thinly sliced

4-cm knob ginger, peeled and thinly sliced

8-cm length cinnamon stick

2 Tbsp meat curry powder

2 Tbsp dried chilli paste

5 red chillies, ground

5 tomatoes, medium-sized, cut into big cubes

1 kg topside beef, cut into pieces

1 Tbsp sugar

Salt to taste

1 beef stock cube

6 Tbsp dark soy sauce

200 ml coconut cream, extracted from 1 grated coconut

250 ml water

4 sprigs mint leaves

METHOD

Heat ghee and cooking oil in a pan over medium heat. Fry curry leaves, onions, garlic, ginger and cinnamon stick until golden brown.

Reduce heat, add meat curry powder, dried chilli paste, ground chillies and tomatoes, and stir well.

Add beef, sugar, salt, beef stock cube, dark soy sauce, coconut cream and water. Stir and add mint leaves. Bring to the boil until meat is tender.

NOTE

Nasi Kandar is a popular dish in Malaysia and is prepared and sold by Indian restaurateurs.

PRAWN SAMBAL
SAMBAL UDANG

INGREDIENTS

4 Tbsp dried chilli paste

8 shallots, peeled and coarsely ground

1 Tbsp dried shrimp paste (*belacan*) powder

125 ml cooking oil

500 g prawns (shrimps), feelers and legs removed

1/2 Tbsp tamarind pulp, mixed with 2 Tbsp water, squeezed and juice strained

6 Tbsp coconut cream, extracted from 1/2 grated coconut

Sugar and salt to taste

METHOD

Combine dried chilli paste, ground shallots and dried shrimp paste in a bowl and stir well.

Heat cooking oil in a pot for 5 minutes and stir-fry chilli paste mixture until fragrant.

Add prawns, tamarind juice and coconut cream. Stir well.

Season with salt and sugar to taste and keep turning the prawns until done.

Transfer to a serving dish and serve hot.

From top: Beef in Black Sauce; Prawn Sambal.

BEEF IN BLACK SAUCE
DAGING MASAK HITAM

INGREDIENTS

100 ml cooking oil

3 onions, peeled and sliced

500 g beef sirloin, cut to desired size but not too small

Salt and sugar to taste

2 red chillies, halved lengthwise

2 green chillies, halved lengthwise

FINELY GROUND

2 sprigs curry leaves

8 shallots, peeled

5 cloves garlic, peeled

3-cm knob mature ginger, peeled

2 Tbsp dried chilli paste

2 Tbsp meat curry powder

8-cm length cinnamon stick

SAUCE (MIXED)

4 Tbsp dark soy sauce

125 ml coconut cream, extracted from $1/2$ grated coconut, if desired

1 tsp tamarind pulp, mixed with 50 ml water, squeezed and juice strained

METHOD

Heat cooking oil in a pan. Fry onions until golden brown. Drain and set aside.

In the same oil, fry ground ingredients until fragrant. Add beef and stir over medium heat until meat is tender.

Add sauce, stirring well until gravy thickens.

Season with salt and sugar to taste before adding red and green chillies together with the fried onions. Stir until chillies soften.

Dish out to a serving plate.

FRIED TILAPIA WITH LEMON BUTTER SAUCE
IKAN TILAPIA GORENG BERSOS MENTEGA LEMON

INGREDIENTS

1 kg tilapia, cleaned with salt water and deboned

1/8 tsp salt

1/2 tsp ground white pepper

80 ml cooking oil

80 g butter

160 g plain (all-purpose) flour

40 g parsley, chopped

LEMON BUTTER SAUCE

160 g butter

1 lemon, juice extracted

Salt to taste

METHOD

TO FRY THE FISH

Rub fish with salt and white pepper and marinate for 5 minutes. Set aside.

Heat cooking oil and butter in a pan.

Coat marinated fish with plain flour and fry in hot oil until done but not too crispy. Remove fish and drain on an absorbent paper.

Arrange fish in a serving dish.

TO PREPARE SAUCE

Melt the butter in a heatproof pan over a low heat.

Add lemon juice and salt and stir until well-combined.

TO SERVE

Pour lemon butter sauce over prepared fish.

Garnish with parsley before serving.

NOTE
This dish is not a Malay heritage dish, but it is one of my favourites nonetheless.

PINEAPPLE AND DRIED SALTED FISH CURRY
GULAI LEMAK NANAS IKAN MASIN

INGREDIENTS

4 dried salted snakeskin gouramy (*ikan sepat)*

250 ml + 100 ml water

200 ml coconut cream, extracted from 1 grated coconut

1/2 pineapple, semi ripe, skinned and cut into 1.5-cm thick pieces

Salt to taste

FINELY GROUND

10 bird's eye chillies (*cili padi*)

8 dried chillies, boiled to soften

2 shallots, peeled

1 clove garlic, peeled

3-cm knob fresh turmeric, peeled

METHOD

Combine fish and ground ingredients in a pot. Add 250 ml water and stir well. Cook over medium heat until the liquid is almost dry.

Add coconut cream and 100 ml water. Stir well. Add pineapple slices and season with salt to taste.

Reduce the heat and allow to boil slowly and stir continuously to avoid oil from separating.

From top: Pineapple and Dried Salted Fish Curry; Fried Tilapia with Lemon Butter Sauce.

SEAWATER CATFISH, BILIMBI AND BITTER GOURD CURRY
GULAI IKAN SEMBILANG, BELIMBING BULUH DAN PERIA KATAK

INGREDIENTS

1 kg seawater catfish
(*ikan sembilang*), scored

250 ml water

2 pieces dried sour fruit
(*asam gelugur*)

500 ml coconut cream,
extracted from 2 grated
coconuts

500 g bilimbi fruits
(*belimbing buluh*)

500 g bitter gourds, small
variety (*peria katak*), halved
and seeded

2 tomatoes, wedged

1 tsp salt

FINELY GROUND

15 bird's eye chillies
(*cili padi*)

1-cm knob fresh turmeric,
peeled

METHOD

Place the catfish and ground ingredients in a pot. Add water and cook for 15 minutes over low heat until boiling.

Add dried sour fruit and coconut cream while stirring slowly. Increase the heat a little and simmer until gravy thickens.

Add the bilimbi fruits, bitter gourds and tomatoes. Season with salt.

Turn off the heat and serve.

NOTE

Use coarse salt and lime juice to clean seawater catfish, then rinse with water. The catfish can be substituted with Spanish mackerel (*ikan tenggiri*).

Usually, the catfish is seasoned with ground turmeric / pounded fresh turmeric and salt mixture, then grilled over a charcoal heat before cooking it in the curry.

CHICKEN KERUTUB
KERUTUB AYAM

INGREDIENTS

250 ml cooking oil

250 ml coconut cream, extracted from 1 grated coconut

1 chicken, about 1.5 kg, cut into pieces

1 Tbsp tamarind pulp, mixed with 2 Tbsp water, squeezed and juice strained

Salt and sugar to taste

WHOLE SPICES (FOR FRYING)

4 cloves

4-cm length cinnamon stick

5 cardamom pods

FINELY GROUND

2 Tbsp dried chilli paste

2 Tbsp pounded roasted grated coconut (kerisik*)

10 shallots, peeled

4 cloves garlic, peeled

2-cm knob ginger, peeled

2-cm knob galangal, peeled

1 Tbsp dried shrimp paste (belacan) powder

25 g meat curry powder

125 g kurma curry powder

METHOD

Heat cooking oil in a pot over medium heat. Fry whole spices until fragrant. Add ground ingredients and stir-fry until aromatic and oil separates.

Add coconut cream and chicken. Cook until boiling and chicken is tender.

Add tamarind juice and season with salt and sugar. Leave to boil and cook until gravy thickens.

NOTE

* Kerisik is made by dry-frying grated coconut until golden brown. Then the coconut is pounded or ground in an electric mill until fine and oily.

From top: Chicken Kerutub; Seawater Catfish, Bilimbi and Bitter Gourd Curry.

GRILLED LEG OF LAMB
KAKI KAMBING PANGGANG

INGREDIENTS

Cooking oil for frying

1 leg of lamb, deboned

Salt to taste

MARINADE (GROUND INTO
   A PASTE)

30 cloves garlic, peeled

5 Tbsp mustard

6 Tbsp tomato sauce

2 Tbsp dried thyme

200 ml olive oil

METHOD

Preheat oven to 170°C.

Season the marinade with salt to taste. Spread evenly on the leg of lamb and leave to marinate for 30 minutes.

Heat cooking oil for frying in a pan. Add marinated leg of lamb and turn over a few times.

Remove leg of lamb from pan and place on baking tray. Grill in the oven for 30 minutes.

Remove grilled leg of lamb and leave to cool for 30 minutes before slicing.

Arrange sliced pieces of the lamb on a plate and serve with mint sauce readily available from the supermarket.

NOTE
This dish is not traditional Malay food but is included in the book because it is one of my favourite dishes.

HOT AND SPICY BEEF
DAGING API-API

INGREDIENTS

125 ml cooking oil

2 Tbsp sugar

1 kg beef rump, sliced
    into 2 x 4 cm and boiled
    until tender

350 ml water

1 Tbsp tamarind pulp,
    mixed with 2 Tbsp water,
    squeezed and juice
    strained

3 Tbsp thick sweet soy sauce

Salt to taste

Coarsely ground black
    peppercorns

COARSELY GROUND

30 dried chillies, boiled
    to soften

15 shallots, peeled

6 cloves garlic, peeled

1 Tbsp black peppercorns

METHOD

Heat cooking oil in a pot over high heat.

Fry ground ingredients until fragrant. Stir and reduce heat.
Add sugar and continue to stir until mixture looks glossy.

Add boiled beef, turning it constantly, and pour in the water,
tamarind juice, thick sweet soy sauce and salt to taste. Cook
until gravy thickens. Remove from heat.

Sprinkle with coarsely ground black pepper before serving.

NOTE
This dish goes well with steamed glutinous rice or plain steamed white
rice or bread.

From top: Grilled Leg of Lamb; Hot and Spicy Beef.

THE FIVE AUNTS' BEEF CURRY
GULAI DAGING MAK CIK BERLIMA

INGREDIENTS

1 kg beef trimmings
(*daging tetelan*)

2 stalks lemon grass, bruised

3 shallots, peeled and sliced

2 cloves garlic, peeled
and sliced

1 tsp fresh turmeric paste

1 Tbsp bird's eye chilli
(*cili padi*) paste

1 Tbsp meat curry powder

1 Tbsp ground dried chillies

Salt to taste

500 ml water

250 ml coconut cream,
extracted from 2 grated
coconuts

METHOD

In a pot, combine beef trimmings, lemon grass, shallots, garlic, turmeric and bird's eye chilli paste, meat curry powder, ground dried chillies, salt and water. Mix well.

Bring to the boil over low heat until beef is tender.

Add half of the coconut cream, lower the heat and stir for a while.

Pour in the remaining coconut cream and continue to cook until the gravy thickens. Turn off the heat.

THAI STYLE SALAD
SALAD SIAM

INGREDIENTS

400 g beef sirloin

Cooking oil for deep-frying

1 aubergine (eggplant/
   brinjal), long variety

SLICED

2 stalks lemon grass

5 red chillies

5 green chillies

6 shallots, peeled

3 sprigs coriander leaves
   (cilantro)

3 sprigs sweet basil leaves
   (*daun selasih*)

SAUCE (MIXED)

3 Tbsp fish sauce (*nampla*)

5 Tbsp lime juice

2 Tbsp brown sugar

6 Tbsp coconut cream,
   extracted from 1/2 grated
   coconut

Salt to taste

METHOD

Slice beef thinly and deep-fry in hot cooking oil for
2 minutes and drain on absorbent paper.

Slice aubergine thinly and dry-fry in a hot frying pan (skillet)
until burn marks appear.

Combine sliced ingredients with aubergine and beef in a
bowl and mix well.

Pour in sauce and mix until well-combined.

Transfer to a serving dish and serve immediately.

NOTE

If you prefer a spicier salad, substitute red and green chillies with bird's
eye chillies (*cili padi*).

From top: The Five Aunts' Beef Curry; Thai Style Salad.

From top: Muscovy Duck Kuzi; Thai Style Chicken.

MUSCOVY DUCK KUZI
KUZI ITIK SERATI

INGREDIENTS

1 Muscovy duck (*itik serati*), about 1.5 kg, cut into 16 pieces

125 ml cooking oil

4 Tbsp *kuzi* spice powder, ready-to-use

4 Tbsp tomato sauce

1 kg onions, peeled, deep-fried and ground

450 ml evaporated milk

1 Tbsp condensed milk

750 ml water

Salt and sugar to taste

FINELY GROUND

20 shallots, peeled

5 cloves garlic, peeled

5-cm knob mature ginger, peeled

METHOD

Mix duck and ground ingredients until well-combined. Marinate for 1 hour.

Heat cooking oil in a deep pan over medium heat. Add *kuzi* spice powder, tomato sauce and ground fried onions. Stir-fry until fragrant.

Add marinated duck and mix well. Stir in evaporated milk, condensed milk and water. Season with salt and sugar to taste. Cook until duck is tender.

Turn off the heat and serve with steamed white rice.

NOTE
Kuzi spice powder is easily available in grocery shops in Kelantan.

THAI STYLE CHICKEN
AYAM BUMBU SIAM

INGREDIENTS

2 Tbsp chicken stock granules

1 Tbsp lime juice

1 Tbsp palm sugar (*gula Melaka*) or brown sugar

Salt to taste

500 g chicken, skinned and cut into large pieces

Cooking oil for frying

10 satay sticks (wooden/ bamboo skewers)

FINELY GROUND

20 bird's eye chillies (*cili padi*)

3 stalks lemon grass

5 shallots, peeled

3 cloves garlic, peeled

4 sprigs coriander leaves (cilantro) with roots

1 tsp ground coriander, dry-fried until fragrant

1 tsp ground fennel, dry-fried until fragrant

1 tsp ground cumin, dry-fried until fragrant

VEGETABLES

1/2 pineapple, skinned and cut into 3 x 3 cm cubes

2 onions, peeled and cut into 3 x 3 cm pieces

1 green capsicum (bell pepper), seeded and thickly sliced

1 red capsicum (bell pepper), seeded and thickly sliced

5 tomatoes, halved

METHOD

Combine all ground ingredients with chicken stock granules, lime juice, palm or brown sugar and enough salt. Add chicken and mix until well-combined.

Heat cooking oil in a frying pan (skillet) and fry chicken and vegetables separately for a few seconds until golden brown.

Thread chicken pieces and alternate with vegetables on the satay sticks. For example, thread green capsicum, followed by chicken, then onion, chicken, red capsicum, chicken and tomato.

To add flavour to the food, transfer the satay sticks to a baking tray and roast in a preheated oven at 170°C for 20 minutes.

Remove the satay from the oven to a serving dish and serve hot.

OX LIVER IN COCONUT MILK CURRY
GULAI HATI LEMBU

INGREDIENTS

150 ml cooking oil

5 sprigs curry leaves

500 ml water

4 potatoes, peeled and cut into big cubes

1 kg ox liver, sliced

200 ml coconut cream, extracted from 1 grated coconut

Salt to taste

SLICED

2 onions, peeled

5 cloves garlic, peeled

3-cm knob ginger, peeled

FINELY GROUND

10 shallots, peeled

6 cloves garlic, peeled

3-cm knob mature ginger, peeled

1 tsp fennel seeds

1 tsp black peppercorns

SPICES (MIXED INTO A PASTE)

5 Tbsp meat curry powder

1 Tbsp ground dried chillies

250 ml water

METHOD

Heat cooking oil in a pan over medium heat. Fry sliced ingredients together with curry leaves until fragrant. Add ground ingredients and stir-fry until aromatic.

Add spice paste and stir well until oil separates.

Pour in 250 ml water and stir. Reduce heat and allow to simmer. Stir in the remaining water and leave to boil.

Put in potatoes and cook until almost tender.

Add ox liver, coconut cream and simmer for 15 minutes over low heat. Season with salt to taste, turn off heat and serve.

NOTE

Ensure liver is not overcooked as it will become hard.

This dish is delicious when eaten with steamed yellow glutinous rice.

ROAST POTATO WITH MINCED CHICKEN FILLING
UBI KENTANG PANGGANG BERINTI AYAM

INGREDIENTS

6 potatoes

300 g minced chicken

5 Tbsp soy beans, soaked overnight and coarsely pounded

8 Tbsp olive oil

5 cloves garlic, peeled and finely chopped

1½ tsp black peppercorns, coarsely ground

3 onions, medium-sized, peeled and finely diced

Salt to taste

250 g grated Cheddar cheese

1 Tbsp fresh rosemary, chopped

METHOD

Boil potatoes with skin until soft. Cut into half lengthwise and scoop out the flesh into a bowl. Set aside the skin.

Preheat oven to 180°C.

Combine potato flesh, minced chicken, soy beans, olive oil, garlic, black pepper, onions and salt. Mix thoroughly and fill each potato skin with the potato mixture.

Combine grated Cheddar cheese and rosemary. Sprinkle over the stuffed potatoes.

Place stuffed potatoes on a baking tray lined with baking paper. Bake in the centre of the oven for 15 minutes until stuffing is cooked.

NOTE

This is also not Malay heritage cuisine, but I love this dish and wish to share it with my readers.

OX TRIPE AND BAMBOO SHOOT CURRY
GULAI PERUT LEMBU DAN REBUNG

INGREDIENTS

4 Tbsp cooking oil

2 Tbsp meat curry powder

2 Tbsp dried chilli paste

2 Tbsp pounded roasted
   grated coconut (*kerisik**)

500 g ox tripe, ready-to-use
   and cut as desired

250 g fresh bamboo shoots,
   cleaned and cut as desired

1 piece dried sour fruit
   (*asam gelugur*)

750 ml water

125 ml coconut cream,
   extracted from 1 grated
   skinned coconut

Sugar and salt to taste

FINELY GROUND

1.25-cm knob ginger, peeled

3 cloves garlic, peeled

5 shallots, peeled

1 stalk lemon grass, sliced

METHOD

Heat cooking oil in a pan and fry ground ingredients for
5 minutes until fragrant.

Add meat curry powder, chilli paste, pounded roasted
grated coconut, ox tripe, bamboo shoots and dried sour fruit.
Stir thoroughly.

Stir in water and cook until gravy thickens. Pour in coconut
cream and continue to cook for 7 minutes until the tripe and
bamboo shoots are tender.

Serve with steamed white rice and other dishes.

NOTE

For the aroma, you can add kaffir lime leaves (*daun limau purut*)
to this dish.

This version is from the state of Perlis, a northern state in
Peninsular Malaysia.

* *Kerisik* is made by dry-frying grated coconut until golden brown. Then
the coconut is pounded or ground in an electric mill until fine and oily.

STEAMED CHICKEN
AYAM KUKUS

INGREDIENTS

1 chicken, about 1.5 kg

3 Tbsp coarse salt

2 chicken stock cubes, crushed

1 tsp sesame oil

1 tsp salt

10-cm knob mature ginger, peeled and pounded

4 spring onions (scallions), knotted

5 sprigs coriander leaves (cilantro) with roots

1 tsp ground white pepper

1 Tbsp oyster sauce

1 litre water

METHOD

Rub chicken with coarse salt. Soak in water for 10 minutes and rinse until clean.

Spread the chicken stock cubes and sesame oil all over the chicken. Rub the insides of chicken with 1 tsp salt.

Stuff the chicken with ginger, spring onions and coriander leaves with the roots. Place chicken in a heatproof container.

Steam over rapidly boiling water for 45 minutes until chicken is cooked.

Serve with chilli sauce of your choice.

From top: Ox Tripe and Bamboo Shoot Curry; Steamed Chicken and two types of chilli sauce.

FRIED SEPANG CAKE
KUIH SEPANG GORENG

INGREDIENTS

3 banana leaves

Cooking oil for deep-frying

DOUGH

500 g glutinous rice flour

A pinch of salt

200 ml water

FILLING

1 coconut, skinned
and grated

250 g palm sugar (*gula Melaka*), finely chopped

200 g granulated sugar

100 ml water

1 screwpine (pandan) leaf,
shredded

METHOD

To prepare the dough, sieve the glutinous rice flour and salt in a mixing bowl. Make a well in the centre and add water a little at a time while mixing slowly until a soft dough is formed. If the dough is still hard, add a little water to make it softer. Set aside.

To make the filling, heat a pan over low heat. Add all the ingredients for the filling and stir until dry. Leave to cool.

To make the cake, take a piece of the dough, about the size of a grade-A egg. Form into a ball and flatten slightly to 1-cm thick on a banana leaf lightly greased with cooking oil.

Place 1 teaspoonful of filling into each dough piece. Fold dough into half to cover the filling. Press the edges of the dough to seal. Repeat the process until all the dough and filling are used up.

Heat cooking oil in a deep pan for deep-frying. Fry cakes until done. Remove and drain. Serve while the cakes are still hot.

NOTE

Be careful when frying glutinous rice dough as it may cause the hot oil to splatter.

These cakes can also be steamed. Just arrange the cakes in a heatproof container lined with banana leaf. Pour 250 ml thick coconut milk seasoned with salt over the cakes. Steam for 20 minutes until cooked.

EGG DODOL
DODOL TELUR

INGREDIENTS

50 egg yolks

375 g butter

375 g granulated sugar

1 screwpine (pandan) leaf, shredded and knotted

Glacé cherries for topping

METHOD

Beat egg yolks in a pot until frothy. Add butter, sugar and screwpine leaf. Stir well.

Bring to the boil over medium heat until cooked, stirring continuously to prevent mixture from turning lumpy.

Remove from heat and pour *dodol* into a container. Discard screwpine leaf. Leave to cool.

Store *dodol* in the refrigerator and serve cold topped with glacé cherries.

From top: Egg Dodol; Fried Sepang Cake.

GOLDEN LACES
JALA EMAS

INGREDIENTS

880 ml water

1 kg sugar

3 screwpine (pandan) leaves, knotted

10 egg yolks

Banana leaf to shape into a cone

METHOD

Boil water, sugar and screwpine leaves in a pot.

Beat egg yolks until frothy.

Hold the banana leaf cone over the boiling syrup and pour egg yolk into the cone. Move the cone in a circular motion to produce lacy yolks in the syrup. Cook for 2 seconds until the golden laces are cooked.

Remove laces using perforated ladle and drain.

NOTE

Switch off the heat while drizzling the egg yolk into the syrup. When all the egg yolks in the cone, are finished, switch on the heat again. Don't over cook the laces as it will harden.

Prepare hot water to be added to the syrup which will thicken while cooking the golden laces.

You can also use the lacy pancake (*roti jala*) cup to drizzle the egg yolks into the syrup.

RICE CAKE IN COCONUT MILK SAUCE AND SYRUP
LOMPAT TIKAM

INGREDIENTS

CAKE

300 g rice flour, sifted

150 g plain (all-purpose) flour, sifted

1.1 litres water

1/2 tsp alkaline water

250 ml screwpine (pandan) juice, extracted from 5 finely pounded screwpine leaves and 250 ml water

SYRUP

220 g brown sugar

440 g granulated sugar

750 ml water

COCONUT MILK SAUCE

600 ml coconut milk, extracted from 1 grated skinned coconut and 550 ml water

50 ml water

1/2 tsp salt

METHOD

TO COOK THE CAKE

Combine cake ingredients in a pot and stir over medium heat.

When mixture becomes thick and shiny, remove from heat and pour into a container or mould measuring 20 x 20 cm that has been chilled in the refrigerator for 1 hour.

Allow cake to cool completely before cutting as desired.

TO COOK THE SYRUP

Combine syrup ingredients in a pot and cook over medium heat until it thickens.

Strain into a bowl and set aside.

TO COOK THE COCONUT MILK SAUCE

Combine coconut milk sauce ingredients in a pot and stir over medium heat until cooked and boiling. Set aside.

TO SERVE

Place cake pieces into individual small bowls.

Pour coconut milk sauce over the cakes and add syrup to taste.

BANANA IN RICH AND SWEET SAUCE
PENGAT PISANG

INGREDIENTS

20 bananas, *Abu* variety

500 g palm sugar (*gula Melaka*), chopped

200 g brown sugar

2 screwpine (pandan) leaves, shredded and knotted

500 ml water

500 ml coconut cream, extracted from 2 grated coconuts

Salt to taste

METHOD

Peel bananas, halve lengthwise and cut into two. Set aside.

Place palm and brown sugars, screwpine leaves and water in a pot. Bring to the boil over medium heat until sugars dissolve. Strain syrup into another pot and add in bananas. Simmer for a while until cooked.

Stir in coconut cream and salt to taste. Stir well to prevent coconut milk from curdling.

Serve as dessert after lunch or dinner.

*From top: Banana in Rich and Sweet Sauce;
Sweet Durian-Flavoured Glutinous Rice.*

SWEET DURIAN-FLAVOURED GLUTINOUS RICE
WAJIK DURIAN

INGREDIENT

1 kg glutinous rice

500 g granulated sugar

500 g brown sugar

250 ml water

500 ml coconut cream, extracted from 2 grated coconuts

2 screwpine (pandan) leaves, shredded and knotted

500 g durian flesh

A pinch of salt

METHOD

Clean glutinous rice and soak for 6 hours. Drain.

Place glutinous rice in a steamer tray and steam for 30 minutes until done. Leave to cool.

Put granulated and brown sugars in a pot. Add water and cook over medium heat until sugars dissolve. Strain syrup into a clean pot.

Add coconut cream to the syrup. Mix in screwpine leaves and cook until very thick and shiny.

Stir in glutinous rice along with the durian flesh and salt. Stir well until dry.

Place mixture in a container lined with banana leaf and compress. Let it cool completely before cutting into pieces.

Serve the cake for afternoon tea.

NOTE

If using 'milk' glutinous rice (*pulut susu*), do not soak the rice. Just clean the rice and steam it straight away.

KATO CAKE
KUIH KATO

INGREDIENTS

250 g brown sugar

1 Tbsp water

500 g glutinous rice flour,
  sifted

125 g rice flour, sifted

5 screwpine (pandan) leaves,
  pounded and mixed with
  75 ml water, squeezed and
  juice strained

750 ml water

125 g grated skinned
  coconut, mixed with a
  pinch of salt and steamed
  for 5 minutes

METHOD

Boil brown sugar and 1 tablespoon water in a pot until sugar
dissolves. Strain into a bowl and set aside.

In a mixing bowl, combine glutinous rice and rice flours,
screwpine juice and 750 ml water. Stir until batter is smooth
and not lumpy. Strain into a baking tin measuring 20 x 20 cm.

Steam over rapidly boiling water for 30 minutes until done.
Remove from steamer and leave to cool completely before
cutting into pieces.

Cut cake into smaller pieces as desired. Roll cake pieces into
steamed grated coconut and arrange on a serving plate.

Pour syrup over and serve.

From top: Kato Cake; King's Pudding.

KING'S PUDDING
PUDING RAJA

INGREDIENTS

200 ml cooking oil

500 g sweet Pahang
   bananas, peeled

100 g glacé cherries

100 g cashew nuts

CUSTARD

1 can evaporated milk

5 egg yolks, lightly beaten

250 g granulated sugar

1 tsp vanilla essence

METHOD

Heat cooking oil in a pan. Fry bananas until golden brown. Remove and drain. Arrange bananas on a serving plate.

To make the custard, boil evaporated milk with egg yolks, sugar and vanilla essence until sauce thickens slightly.

Pour sauce over prepared bananas and sprinkle with glacé cherries and cashew nuts before serving.

NOTE

This pudding is best served with Golden Laces (see recipe on page 88). Spread the golden laces on the fried bananas after pouring the sauce over and then top with glacé cherries and cashew nuts.

Usually, dried prunes are used to garnish this pudding.

Ingredients

Spices

Cardamom

Coriander

Cumin

Dried shrimp paste

Fennel

Fenugreek

Star anise

Tamarind pulp

Chillies

Dried sour fruit slices
(*asam gelugur*)

Galangal

Turmeric

Dry Ingredients

Basmati rice

Dried prawns (shrimps)

Lotus seeds

Masoor dhall

Mung bean dhall

Palm sugar (*gula Melaka*)

Rice

Urud dhall

Vegetables

Aubergine
(eggplant/brinjal)

Bitter gourd, small variety
(peria katak)

Chinese mushrooms

Ladies' fingers

Oyster mushrooms

Parkia/stink beans *(petai)*

Parkia/stink bean pods

Potatoes

Flavouring & Herbs

Chinese chives

Coriander leaves (cilantro)

Curry leaves

Kaffir lime leaves
(daun limau purut)

Kalamansi

Lemon grass

Lime

Pennywort *(pegaga)*

Polygonum leaves
(daun kesum)

Sweet basil leaves
(daun selasih)

Torch ginger bud
(bunga kantan)

Turmeric leaves

Weights and Measures

Quantities for this book are given in metric measures.
Standard measurements used are: 1 tsp = 5 ml, 1 Tbsp = 15 ml, 1 cup = 250 ml.
All measures are level unless otherwise stated.

LIQUID AND VOLUME MEASURES

Metric	Imperial	American
5 ml	$1/6$ fl oz	1 teaspoon
10 ml	$1/3$ fl oz	1 dessertspoon
15 ml	$1/2$ fl oz	1 tablespoon
60 ml	2 fl oz	$1/4$ cup (4 tablespoons)
85 ml	$2^1/2$ fl oz	$1/3$ cup
90 ml	3 fl oz	$3/8$ cup (6 tablespoons)
125 ml	4 fl oz	$1/2$ cup
180 ml	6 fl oz	$3/4$ cup
250 ml	8 fl oz	1 cup
300 ml	10 fl oz ($1/2$ pint)	$1^1/4$ cups
375 ml	12 fl oz	$1^1/2$ cups
435 ml	14 fl oz	$1^3/4$ cups
500 ml	16 fl oz	2 cups
625 ml	20 fl oz (1 pint)	$2^1/2$ cups
750 ml	24 fl oz ($1^1/5$ pints)	3 cups
1 litre	32 fl oz ($1^3/5$ pints)	4 cups
1.25 litres	40 fl oz (2 pints)	5 cups
1.5 litres	48 fl oz ($2^2/5$ pints)	6 cups
2.5 litres	80 fl oz (4 pints)	10 cups

OVEN TEMPERATURE

	°C	°F	Gas Regulo
Very slow	120	250	1
Slow	150	300	2
Moderately slow	160	325	3
Moderate	180	350	4
Moderately hot	190/200	370/400	5/6
Hot	210/220	410/440	6/7
Very hot	230	450	8
Super hot	250/290	475/550	9/10

LENGTH

Metric	Imperial
0.5 cm	$1/4$ inch
1 cm	$1/2$ inch
1.5 cm	$3/4$ inch
2.5 cm	1 inch

DRY MEASURES

Metric	Imperial
30 grams	1 ounce
45 grams	$1^1/2$ ounces
55 grams	2 ounces
70 grams	$2^1/2$ ounces
85 grams	3 ounces
100 grams	$3^1/2$ ounces
110 grams	4 ounces
125 grams	$4^1/2$ ounces
140 grams	5 ounces
280 grams	10 ounces
450 grams	16 ounces (1 pound)
500 grams	1 pound, $1^1/2$ ounces
700 grams	$1^1/2$ pounds
800 grams	$1^3/4$ pounds
1 kilogram	2 pounds, 3 ounces
1.5 kilograms	3 pounds, $4^1/2$ ounces
2 kilograms	4 pounds, 6 ounces

ABBREVIATION

tsp	teaspoon
Tbsp	tablespoon
g	gram
kg	kilogram
ml	millilitre
cm	centimetre
mm	millimetre